GAMECHANGERS

The Truth About Black Men and Fraternities

DR. CASSANDRA Y. OWENS

DR. NES INTERNATIONAL CONSULTING & PUBLISHING

LOS ANGELES COUNTY, CA

The book recounts certain events in the lives of various individuals according to their recollection and perspective while providing brief histories and overviews of various popular organizations. The goal of their stories is not to defame any person or image or organization, but the sole purpose is to encourage and empower the reader.

Acknowledgements

I wrote this book because I want to encourage a conversation about how the world perceives black men in the United States of America. As early as I could remember, I've always had an affinity towards black men. Their love, their emotional and spiritual stamina, their ingenuity, their resilience have inspired my love and respect for them. I want to use this project to assist others in understanding my pride, my hope is that more people embrace; Black Men in this country. There are many of them that impacted my own life. Some of them I will highlight in the pages that follow. I want to acknowledge and give special thanks to:

Ms. Helen J. Owens, who is always there to encourage and inspire me. Thank you, Mom, for your unconditional love and undying support.

Mr. Richard Snow, who is a good friend who never says "no" when needed.

Dr. Vickie Cox-Edmundson, my soror and friend -can you believe that we are both college professors and published authors?!

Ms. Thomasina Turner-Diggs, who was my college roommate who continuously believes in me when I do not believe in myself. I love you Rhea.

Ms. Rochelle Davis, was my BFF from high school(we remain connected). Your support during this project has been invaluable. Thanks Ro.

Ms. Nicole Bentley, my sista friend who introduced me to the best publisher. Thanks Nikki.

Mrs. Debbie Brown, Ms. Dee Dee Dukes, and Mrs. Letitia Duckett are my prayer partners. Thank you for the early morning prayer sessions. They make a difference!

Bishop Nathaniel Bond and the entire DHP/LLM Family; I love all of you!!!!!

All the Fraternity Executive Directors:
Mr. John Paul   Alpha Phi Alpha Fraternity, Inc.
Mr. John Burrell   Kappa Alpha Psi Fraternity, Inc.
Mr. Kenneth Barnes   Omega Psi Phi Fraternity, Inc.
Mr. Daryl Anderson   Phi Beta Sigma, Fraternity, Inc.
Mr. Kevin Bennett   Iota Phi Theta Fraternity, Inc.

Clark Atlanta University (CAU)- to all the faculty and staff members who poured knowledge into me; my classmates; thank you CAU family for being a safe place for me to make mistakes, learn from them and continue to grow.

Contents

Dr. Cassandra Y. Owens

Blank pages are intentional

Dedication

This book is dedicated to my favorite fraternity man:

My Dad- Dr. Robert G. Owens, Sr.

He is a member of Alpha Phi Alpha Fraternity, Inc.; and he has influenced my life in remarkable ways.

Dad, thank you for always making me feel special, loved, unique, and understood. I appreciate all the secrets that we share; our travel time together and just being in your presence. My favorite memory is seeing my first play on Broadway. It was the Whiz. The buzz around New York was about this 16-year-old girl who was blowing up Broadway. I am so grateful for the exposure and because of the experiences that you provided; I have self-confidence, pride and I stand tall. I love you Dad and thanks for being the best Alpha man I know.
I LOVE YOU, DADDY 🖤

-To Tommie Smith and John Carlos

Dr. Cassandra Y. Owens

PREFACE

---

*B*lack fraternities have historically played a significant role and have been an integral part of the history of this nation since their inception beginning near the turn of the century. While they've provided support to their memberships and the African American communities, they also made major contributions to society in very meaningful ways.

Today these organizations have a combined membership of nearly one million men. This number means that working together they have been able to positively impact most chosen issues or actions.

Most of them have already celebrated their 100th anniversary. This longevity and level of service have historically made them major players in most games in this country.

Despite national prominence and major accomplishments, Black fraternities are often criticized by many in academic circles, improperly portrayed by the media, and misunderstood by non-members. However, it should also be noted that there are some members who question their organizations' relevance and the degree to which they are being guided by their founding principles today.

Pondering these thoughts and my perception of the African American man made me do some reflecting on what brought me to this point.

GAME CHANGERS

Having observed the fraternity men and admiring many of them from a distance, I have always been impressed. However, I realized there was more to my admiration than a stroll show, community service project, or well sung hymn. So, I decided to dig a little deeper.

The year is 2020 in the Unites States of America, the land of the free and the home of the brave. Most people admire this country from afar and view the country as the land of opportunity. Let me be clear, I love this country and I do not want to live anywhere else. However, I often wonder if this country loves me back. Again, the year is 2020 and another young black man is killed for no justifiable reason. And this is not an anomaly. I watched the *Netflix* based documentary *13th* by award winning director Ava Duvernay.

During the dialogue, there was a reference made to the movie *"The Birth of a Nation."* It left me enlightened, but also gasping for air when I consider the systemic narrative that has consistently portrayed black men in a negative way. Their incredulous response to ongoing stereotypes in the media that hypersexualize and, over criminalize black men has been perpetuated for generations.

The 1968 Olympics was a turning point for me. I remember watching the television in the den of my home and seeing two young men on the podium with a raised-fist salute, a symbol of black power. Mr. Tommie Smith and Mr. John Carlos, who had won gold and bronze medals, respectively, stood tall and proud as they sent their message to the world.

They agreed to use their medal wins as an opportunity to highlight the social issues stirring in the United States. Racial tensions were high, and the Black Power movement had been launched as well as the human rights movement at large. I did not understand at the time what the raised fist meant but I knew it must have been something big. I admired them. After I learned what their actions represented that day, my admiration for black men and those men who stood for the cause began to resonate even more.

Smith and Carlos became heroes to a little girl who really did not understand the struggle, but knew it was real. They sought out an active form of protests and advocated for racial pride, black nationalism, and dramatic action rather than incremental change.

It is my understanding that they were banned from participating in any more Olympic Athletic events and they were shunned in this country and lived meager lives because of the actions they had taken that day. During that same time, Mr. James Brown coined the phrase and hit song that has become my personal national anthem, *"Say it Loud, I'm Black and I'm Proud."* I believed it. I knew it. I would later learn, there were many that didn't find reason to believe anything good about black people, particularly black men.

The courage and persistence of two young men changed my life in such a positive and influential way. I am eternally grateful to those brothers for their tenacity and persistence in showing the world the injustices that Black people endured. My love for black men became clear and distinct for me. My parents were intentional about making sure my siblings and I knew about the struggle and injustices that black people faced and what it meant for all of us.

As I continued to do research about black history, another killing stirred national and international media. The torturous murder of Emmett Till in Money, Mississippi caused rage across the world. In fact, his accuser has recanted her story; but the death of Emmett Till still haunts the black community to this day. His mother, Ms. Mamie Till made the decision to funeralize her son with an open casket to show the world how he was brutally beaten, and body parts severed. Is it possible that Mr. Till's death along with countless others, inspired Mr. Smith and Mr. Carlos to take a stand that day? Of that I am not certain, but the unwarranted black deaths have persisted.

Dr. Cassandra Y. Owens

In 2012 the death of Mr. Trayvon Martin, a 17-year-old, killed by a neighborhood watchman while walking home from the convenience store ignited another movement. After Mr. Martin, there was Mr. Eric Gardner, Mr. Tamir Rice, Mr. Michael Brown, Mr. Sean Bell, Mr. Denroy "DJ Henry, Mr. Ahmad Aubrey and Mr. George Floyd. These are some of the ones we know about, many others did not get counted because there were not cameras or witnesses. The US is one of the most advanced countries in the world, yet, still, no advancements have been made regarding the unwarranted killings of black men. We must take a stand. With this work, I hope to inject another perspective of what our country knows about who black men are and what they have collectively accomplished in their communities, and in our nation.

I salute men like Mr. Colin Kaepernick (who is also a fraternity man), who have used their platforms to fight for justice. For me, he is the modern-day Smith and Carolos. It was his protest of killings that propelled forward movement. His courage to kneel and declare that something must change has inspired countless numbers of Americans. Ironically, more than 40 years after Smith and Carlos' fight, Mr. Kaepernick experienced the same fate as Smith and Carlos—loss of job. Why are we repeatedly punished for doing what is right?

All these young Black men who had been either killed or treated badly and then often maligned by the media made me wonder about the voracity of the news we see and hear about our men.

News about fraternity hazing gets much more attention from the media than their community service projects and programming. There is much more to fraternities than hazing. In fact, I have received assistance from instructors and associates who were fraternity men. I have worked with some wonderful fraternity men who went out of their way to ensure my well-being. However, I was intrigued to understand if my perspective about black fraternity men was just personal.

After much research, I understood that it was a part of my responsibility to shift the narrative, and ultimately develop a new narrative specifically as it relates to black men in America who are members of fraternities. Black men are not scary, deranged, confused or insane. The men in the pages of the book have the smarts and the swag. They are men of impact and influence.

GAME CHANGERS

They are scholars, servant leaders, athletes, and businessmen. Black men are appreciated, strong, courageous, fearless, trailblazers, trendsetters, husbands, fathers, and loved by this black woman writing this book and many others in their world. This book is about men who "changed the game."

It is my hope that you learn and walk away with a new wisdom about their multifaceted nature, who black men, are and destined to become.

It is my honor and privilege to highlight some of the lesser known information of Black Men. This evidence-based book proves the power and positive influence that black fraternities have on their campuses and in their communities. Through research and personal stories, this book sheds a new and deserving light on black men everywhere, especially those in fraternities.

Dr. Cassandra Y. Owens

This book is their moment, their time to shine and be celebrated. I am hopeful that as you read this book you will replace the men of my life with the men who influenced you and your communities.

So, enjoy, and I hope the pages of this book begin to change the narrative about black men in the world at large.

BLACK MEN IN AMERICA

1

I am employed at a small private Christian Historically Black College in the state of Tennessee. While attending chapel, a scene occurred that birthed the idea for this book. Chapel was held in the transformed gym. There were students sitting in the bleachers, and there were theater style seats on the floor. There was another section for faculty members. Seated across from the faculty were members of fraternities and sororities. I sat there, thinking about the subject to be taught in my upcoming class. I pondered what I would eat for lunch and began scanning the room amazed by the students that filled the room.

I enjoyed watching underclassmen navigate the campus with a restless demeanor, and after four years of matriculation, they maneuvered the same campus with a sense of authority. I noticed the person at the podium. The young man was dressed in his black suit, white shirt and a black and gold tie. As he gave the campus announcements, the thought struck me, "he is the Student Government President as well as a member of a prestigious fraternity." As I began reflecting, I tabulated the fact that the last six SGA Presidents were also members of that same fraternity (expect one year). I tuned in to the rest of his talk, and I reflected on the fact that while this was something, I had become accustomed to, black male leadership was not viewed as the norm in the rest of society. These men were true campus leaders. They had not been accused of hazing, or orchestrating wild parties, or any kind of demeaning behavior.

In fact, these young men were and are leaders, excelling in their academics and destined to do great things.

However, when we think or discuss African American men who are fraternity members their positive stories are rarely reported. Hence, it has become my duty to switch the narrative, and highlight the stories less shared about the incredible impact these men are having on their campuses and in society at large.

Fast forward a couple of years. When I entered graduate school to earn a doctorate degree, my professor inquired about my topic of study. Immediately I knew, it was going to have something to do with the subject of African American males and their involvement with Historically Black Colleges and Universities (HBCUs).

Over the course of time, I settled on this topic: "The impact of fraternity involvement on leadership skills, academic success, and interaction with peers, faculty, and staff of African American Males at Historically Black Colleges and Universities."

It was my contention that few studies existed that emphasized the positive life of fraternity involvement for African American males at Historically Black Colleges and Universities. When their is a discussion on African American fraternities, the conversation centers around the problems with hazing, drinking, and low-grade point averages while moving through the initiation process. I in no way want to pretend that those problems do not exist among fraternity life. However, the purpose of this book is to tell the stories of African American males who are involved in fraternities who are excelling and have contributed to this society in great ways.

So, I decided that the stories of this populace needed to be told and hopefully we can change the narrative when discussing African American males.

Now, I want to lay a foundation regarding my own background. Both of my parents were educators; so, I was determined that I would not follow in their footsteps.

My dad, a member of Alpha Phi Alpha Fraternity, was employed at Lane College during my childhood. He taught music and was director of the College concert choir. He received the Doctor of Musical Arts from Memphis State University when I was around the age of sixteen. Since that time, he has held multiple positions as faculty and administrator holding the position of Chair of the department of Performing and Fine Arts. My mom whom he met at Lane College, held positions of teacher, principal, and evaluator of teachers and principals for the state of Tennessee.

Not only were my parents' leaders in the field of education, they were active and leaders in several civic organizations.

Like the "preacher's kid" I was the "professor's kid." My brothers and I were born when my parents were living in the "faculty apartments." Could that be a sign? I knew all his students, attended every athletic event, concert choir performance, fraternity and sorority step and probate show and anything else that was happening on campus.

Each year after the choir's Christmas performance my mom would prepare a large meal. The choir members would come to our house to eat and just spend time with our family. I really enjoyed this. Spending time on the campus interacting with the college students was special to me. So much so, that from a young age, I was anticipating my arrival at college. Preferably, it would be a small, private, church-related primarily African American college like Lane.

I attended Clark College located in Atlanta, GA. I majored in Business Administration with a concentration in Marketing. I was an average student. Now I know that a business degree probably should not have been my first choice, but I made it work. I graduated and found work in my area. While few of these jobs were lasting or gave me much intrinsic satisfaction, I gained something from each one that helped me become the professional who gets along well with most colleagues and students. After a divorce, I moved to North Carolina where my parents had relocated since all their children were adults.

I took a job at Fayetteville State University in the Office of Financial Aid. For the next ten years I stayed in this area working my way up to Director of the Financial Aid Office at two colleges. Working in Student Personnel Services provided me the opportunity to work with students from all academic sectors, and with varying academic interests and resources.

This was the beginning of my realization that higher education was the place where I probably wanted to spend the rest of my professional life.

It is for the reasons above that I have an indelible love for historically black colleges and universities. Historically Black Colleges and Universities (HBCUs) are institutions of higher education in the United States that were established before 1964 with the intention of serving the black community. A church group or denomination founded most of the private institutions; those private colleges still boast of the connection and relationship with the mother or founding church.

Discussions on the relevance of Historically Black Colleges and Universities continue to exist; it has been suggested the HBCUs are no longer relevant and their purpose is now outdated and unnecessary. Albritton (2012) gives comprehensive reasons to prove the validity of these institutions. HBCUs are still havens of learning for the disadvantaged students of color. The achievement gap in K-12 learning is reported to be narrowing, but it still exists. Even minority students who end up graduating from high school drop out of college at higher rates than their white counterparts. HBCU's have been able to succeed with large numbers of these students. HBCUs are blazing successful STEM trials with minority students. HBCU's are important hubs for developing the greatest STEM minds in the nation, with 65% of all Black physicians and half of all Black engineers graduating from HBCUs. Another interesting fact is the financial assistance provided to most students who attend.

Many HBCUs have an inherent understanding that large numbers of their students come from a place where college may not be an option without sound financial advice. These institutions provide the means to make college affordable for this cadre of students.

As college costs climb, HBCUs remain options for earning degrees for students with meager resources. They adequately staff the workforce and help graduates find jobs. Finally, today's HBCUs remind us that there are still battles to be fought. Diversity is a good thing, but there is a sense of solidarity obtained at HBCUs that needs to be retained. Despite legislation and litigation against discrimination, it is important to remember that the fight for civil rights and equity is still a reality. It is vital to remember why the HBCU was developed in the first place and what role they have played in the fight for justice.

Though the initial mission of HBCUs may have evolved, the reminder that education is an inalienable right for all Americans and those that choose to study from abroad, lives on proudly at HBCUs and will always be a necessary pillar of the US college and university system.

THE CASE OF BLACK MALES IN COLLEGIATE ENVIRONMENTS

Although African Americans continue to demonstrate a desire for education, African American male enrollment and completion rates in higher education continue to be lower when compared to other ethnic groups. Despite these overall trends, many African American males have been successful in becoming engaged and persisting to the completion of their undergraduate studies.

Developing an understanding of how and why some black males avoid the pitfalls and hardships plagued by others may assist in devising ways to protect and support African American males while in college and offer strategies and activities that may encourage achievement (Noguera, 2003).

There has been controversy within the academic community on the potential benefits from fraternity involvement, and covertly there has been speculation on whether the college Greek system adheres to its stated tenets of scholarship, brotherhood, and leadership. Kuh, Pascarella, and Wechsler (1996) stated: "almost monthly, a college or university fraternity makes the national news because of an escapade of underage drinking or a hazing episode resulting in bodily injury or worse" (p.1). In fact, many incidents of this sort create a need for at least one law firm that specializes in fraternity-related lawsuits. Some have contended the undesirable attention focused on the academy because of such unpleasant activities has created a climate of questioning the significance of Greek-letter organizations.

Others have questioned the value of tolerating such potential sources for embarrassment.

THE CASE FOR BLACK FRATERNITIES

In contrast, Greek life and membership in African American Greek-lettered fraternities provide African American men many opportunities to gain valuable leadership experience. Members of these organizations often engage in tutoring, mentoring, community service, and promote a sense of belonging among their members (Harper, 2008; Ross, 2000). These organizations have academic standards in place to ensure each chapter maintains good academic standing, allowing them to operate on campus. Given their multitude of benefits, Greek letter organizations could be utilized as a recruitment tool and a mechanism for increased student retention.

McClure (2006b) found that membership in African American Greek Letter Fraternities help African American men build connections while creating a 'niche' to address their needs and experiences.

Graham (1999) indicated that fraternities provide a forum, post-college, through which some of the best-educated African Americans can discuss an agenda to fight racism and improve conditions for other disadvantaged African Americans. Unlike white collegiate organizations, the African American fraternity experience begins in college, and it is an activity that has even greater importance after graduation. An under-representation of African American males in education has serious repercussions not only for the men themselves, but also for this society. Whenever a group of individuals is not interacting and achieving at optimum levels, the country is robbed of talent that could enrich the lives of many.

Today, having existed for over a century, Black fraternities create an elite social group within the African American community.

These organizations are responsible for producing some of the nation's most prominent Black leaders (Ross, 2000) and the most influential students on college campuses. Yet, the influences of this Greek system on the collegiate experience are not well researched. Most of the existing literature and popular media outlets emphasize negative aspects of Black Greek life such as their rigorous pledging and hazing rituals. Although "Black fraternal organizations are a 'jewel' to many African Americans who revere their heritage, character, history and values" (Nuwer, 1999 p.180) the pledge process/hazing rituals over time have drawn significant negative media attention. Walter Kimbrough (2003a), author of Black Greek 101, and one of the leading contributors to Black Greek literature notes that little has been written that adds to the knowledge of the Black Greek experience.

African American fraternities should be recognized for their emphasis on leadership development and academic success among their membership. Within the boundaries of National Pan-Hellenic Council organizations, there has been appreciation for the efforts to cultivate a responsible civic orientation that is related to fostering leaders for society. While each fraternity has its own unique mission, a common focus for these young men from their inception was to give leadership to struggling people, to pull together the best trained African American minds to lead the community.

Historically, African American fraternities have created a unique culture for their collegiate members, yet their impact on negotiating the perceived climate on college campuses has yet to be explored.

This book will provide a different view of African American Fraternities in hopes of obtaining a better understanding of the effects of these organizations on its African American males.

Dr. Cassandra Y. Owens

The culture of individual campuses has maintained the capacity to positively impact the lives of potential members. Their influences on various members leads to holistic transformation in the lives of each member. And now, I am sharing this information in this book because no woman loves African American men more than I do. I just believe that these men have done great things, accomplished great things, because they are built to last. Despite systemic challenges, in my opinion, African American men still rise to the occasion. So, as you continue to read the next few pages of this book, reflect on the black men that impacted your own life. I am willing to bet that they were members of an African American fraternity.

FRATERNITY MEN YOU KNOW

2

This chapter will test your knowledge of some men you probably know; but what you do not know is that many of the men you already admire and have historical figures are also fraternity men.

Notable men of Alpha Phi Alpha are:

Dr. Martin Luther King, Jr., Mr. Omari Hardwick, Mr. Stuart Scott, Mr. James P. Brawley, Mr. Lionel Ritchie, Justice Thurgood Marshall, Mr. Duke Ellington, Mr. John H. Johnson, Mr. Paul Robeson, Dr. Cornell West,

Dr. Cassandra Y. Owens

Mr. Donny Hathaway, Judge Joe Brown, Mr. Keenan Ivory Wayans, Dr. DuBois, Mr. Walt Frazier, Mr. Roland Martin, Mr. Gerald Albright, Mr. Andrew Young, Mr. Dick Gregory, Mr. Garrett Morgan.

Notable Men of Kappa Alpha Psi include: Coach Penny Hardaway, Mayor Tom Bradley, Pastor Marvin Sapp, Mr. Marc Lamont Hill, Mr. Colin Kaepernick, Mr. John Singleton, Comedian Cedric the Entertainer, Mr. Montell Jordan, Pastor Smokie Norfolk, Mr. Bryon Cage, Mr. Donald Byrd, Mr. Jester Hairston, Mr. Elwood Buchanan, Naledge, Mr. Gerald Alston, Mr. Stan Lathan, Mr. Whitman Mayo, Mr. Thomas "Nephew Tommy Miles", Mr. Tavis Smiley, Mr. Robert L. Johnson, Mr. Carl Ware.

Notable Men of Omega Psi Phi Fraternity include: Mr. William "Count" Basie, Mr. Steve McNair, Mr. Shaquille O'Neil, Dr. Benjamin Mays, Mr. Steve Harvey, Mr. Wanya Morris, Mr. John Salley, Rev.

GAME CHANGERS

Jesse Jackson, Mr. Michael Jordan, Dr. Charles Drew, Mr. Ricky Smiley, Mr. Tom Joyner, Mr. Langston Hughes, Mr. Titus O'Neil, Mr. Vince Carter, Mr. Ronald McNair, Mr. Joe Torry, and Mr. DL Hughley.

Notable Men of Phi Beta Sigma Fraternity include:
Mr. Jerry Rice, Actor Malik Yoba, Actor Terrance Howard, Mr. George Washington Carver, Actor Blair Underwood, Mr. Harry Belafonte, Mr. Bootsy Collins, Mr. Al Roker, Mr. Emmitt Smith, Mr. Les Brown, Mr. A. Philip Randolph, Mr. Karl Malone, Mr. Maurice White, Mr. Vernon White, Mr. Rick James, Dr. Bobby Jones, Mr. Larry Blackmon, Actor Morgan Freeman.

Notable Men of Iota Phi Theta include: actor Terrence Carson, Actor Arnez Hines, II, Actor Manuel Olazabal, Mr. Kendric Dean, and Mr. Spence Christian

Dr. Cassandra Y. Owens

JEWELS ON MY JOURNEY

3

*E*ach of the fraternal organizations of color evolved during a period when African Americans were being denied basic rights and privileges that were granted to others. Being isolated by race on predominantly white campuses and facing racial barriers across society created a need for men of color to unite and align themselves with other individuals who shared common history and aspirations. The Black fraternal movement grew, and leaders emerged who were able to make a difference on campuses and in the communities that they served.

Dr. Cassandra Y. Owens

The sharing of goals and ideals and the need to see them become a reality was one of the threads that made the Black fraternal movement develop as such a strong force in American society. In most communities, they were men who emerged as leaders or spokespersons and often they had been to college and had the benefit afforded them by fraternity membership.

On a personal level, my reflections on my observations,experiences and conversations about Greek life and fraternity men took me to several who profoundly impacted my life. I remember fondly several of the men who inspired me as I was growing up and who continue to do so today because of the level of leadership they exhibited and provide today. As you read this chapter, it is my hope that you can reflect and remember those men, many of whom shared the fraternal bond, who impacted your life's journey. This chapter will highlight the men in my life that I remember who encouraged me or that I admired from a distance.

I will look at the men of three different generations to highlight the real value of fraternity men. They started their journeys near the turn of the 20th century and continue as they rise to meet today's challenges.

Dr. Chester Arthur Kirkendoll
Alpha Phi Alpha Fraternity, Inc.

The first man I remember having adoration for is Bishop Chester Arthur Kirkendoll, a member of Alpha Phi Alpha Fraternity, Inc. Dr. Kirkendoll was president of Lane College when I was born. He was my dad's boss and was always spoken of with near reverence in our home. Although he was my dad's boss, we lived on the campus near the President's home. At that time, the President's home was on the campus. I remember visiting the President's home with my mom. The year was 1964.

Imagine a four or five-year-old little girl walking into a large two-story home, eloquently decorated house, looking around and taking in every detail. Often there was this older man who appeared to be seven feet tall who always spoke to me. He seemed to be aware of my nervousness, and always tried to make me comfortable before he left the room so that the ladies could have their "women talk". The president always gave me a slight smile while keeping the family's black poodle, Inky, at bay. I never remember hearing him speak in public; but I am told he was an outstanding preacher and orator. I often wonder if he is one of the reasons being around men is somewhat comforting to me. I can remember vividly the warmth I felt in his presence. Although I was small, I felt like he was watching me closely and cared greatly about my welfare.

GAME CHANGERS

My personal interactions with this historical giant are minute in comparison to the contributions he made to Lane College, the Christian Methodist Episcopal Church, the Jackson community, and the nation at large. He led Lane College through the turbulent 70's when the African American community was attempting to discover their place in the modern society. I remember that the Science Building, one of the College's best and well equipped, was burned to the ground and President Kirkendoll held his faculty and student body together.

My admiration for this man who stood tall physically, but also as a leader of his times, enlarged as I grew older and learned more about his contributions. During his administration, he added significantly to the physical growth of the campus. Some of his major accomplishments included the completion of the following buildings: J.T. Beck Faculty Apartments, B. Julian Smith Residence Hall, the Kirkendoll Student

Dr. Cassandra Y. Owens

Center, Jubilee Men's Residence Hall, a new Science Building and Hamlett Women's Residence Hall. In 1961, President Kirkendoll provided leadership as the College received full membership in the Southern Association of Colleges and Schools (SACS).

In 1970 he was elected bishop of the Christian Methodist Episcopal Church and assigned to the Third Episcopal District with offices in St. Louis, MO. Ebony Magazine named him one of the 100 most influential African Americans in 1984. This fraternity man recognized the need for solid leadership in the African American community during his time and he used all that he had learned as an Alpha man to ensure that his legacy would continue to live long after he was gone.

Mr. J.A. Cooke
Phi Beta Sigma Fraternity, Inc.

Another fraternity man that impacted my life was, Mr. J.A. Cooke. There was not a chapter of the Phi Beta Sigma Fraternity on the Lane College campus. However, it was widely known that Mr. James A. Cooke, the Athletic Director, football coach, and Dean of Men, was a member of the organization that had its birth in 1914. It is my understanding that he wore it proudly, yet quietly. While three of the hats he wore are mentioned, Mr. Cooke is recalled as one who could be called on at any time for the institution at large or the students he loved.

In the days when HBCUs could not afford to be completely staffed, Mr. Cooke is remembered for recognizing the importance of ensuring that the rules were adhered to and went beyond the call of duty to make sure it happened.

I am told that he could walk into a setting where there was an altercation or major disruption and take charge in three minutes. His former students suggest that the Lane College students had enough respect and fear of him to immediately obey whatever he commanded. However, the football players and other athletes loved him enough to want to win in his honor.

For many years he was the only Phi Beta Sigma man in the area. However, I developed a great deal of respect for the men of Phi Beta Sigma because of J. A. Cook. They define themselves by "Culture, Scholarship, and Service" and his contribution to Lane College and the West Tennessee area resembled just that.

Mr. Clifford Miner
Omega Psi Phi Fraternity, Inc.

Mr. Clifford Miner was my high school Algebra teacher. Mr. Miner was a no nonsense; take no prisoners high school teacher. He had a stern personality that we thought was pretty intense. Students viewed him as a mean teacher; now I know he just wanted us to be the best we could be. I like to think that I adapted some of my teaching acumen from Mr. Miner. He was clear about his assignments and expectations in the classroom. And, so am I.

He graduated from Lane College after spending time in the Navy. I am told he completed his degree in three years. After teaching in Bolivar, TN; he was employed at Merry High School where he taught math for 27 years.

Dr. Cassandra Y. Owens

He became a member of Omega Psi Phi Fraternity while a student at Lane College. Although he was married and had two children and a job, he managed to join the men who wore purple and gold. His leadership skills made him one of the leaders of the local undergraduate and graduate chapters of Omega Psi Phi Fraternity, Inc.

Another interesting aspect of Mr. Miner's contributions was his impact on the part of the African American community called "Mound City" in which he lived. He was a shrewd money manager. He invested in that African American community and others around the city. He would buy and manage property because he understood the principle that we must keep our money and talent in our communities. In 1985, he established Clifford Miner and Associates through which much of his financial development was facilitated. Mr. Miner understood that one of the best ways to advance and help your brothers and sisters is to have ownership.

As I reflect on Mr. Miner's influence on my life, I recognize that his true character was defined by his convictions, the choices he made, and the promises he kept. As I knew him, he held to his principles, and refused to be swayed by the winds of convenience. What he said and what he did were congruent and defined who he was. I believe that much of that was learned through his membership in the Omega Psi Phi Fraternity.

Dr. Leo LaSimba Gray
Omega Psi Phi Fraternity, Inc.

Growing up on the campus of Lane College, I always had a boyfriend. Usually, my boyfriends were members of the choir or Alpha Phi Alpha because they would interact with my dad. Now, these young men did not know that I was their girlfriend; but in my mind they were my boyfriends. I remember clearly at the age of eight deciding that Mr. Leo Gray was my boyfriend.

Leo had a warm smile, dressed nicely to an eight-year-old. He was from Memphis, TN. He is a member of Omega Psi Phi Fraternity, Inc. An interesting note is that since he was not a member of the choir or my dad's fraternity, I do not know how I was able to know him. But, at some point he was in my presence, and I was hooked on Leo Gray.

Leo had several personal characteristics that he brought to college with him that made him stand out from the crowd. He always had a nice haircut. He laughed easily and seemed to make people feel at ease. I gathered that he had some goals already set and was determined to reach them. He made people feel as if he really liked them, even me.

Leo graduated from Lane and moved to St. Louis to teach school for one year. He returned to Lane in the summer of 1969 to become the Director of Alumni Affairs; he was the first person to hold that position on a full-time basis.

In 1973, He left Lane to work at the University of Tennessee Medical school in Memphis where he served as coordinator for Community Outreach for the Sickle Cell Anemia Comprehensive Program.

Dr. Leo LaSimba Gray is Pastor Emeritus of the historic New Sardis Baptist Church in Germantown, Tennessee. He served this congregation for 25 years as Senior Pastor. During his tenure at New Sardis, the membership grew by 2000 members. Dr. Gray constructed a new edifice that includes a historic museum that tells the history of the Civil Rights Movement. It was my pleasure to minister for him on several occasions and I still enjoy going to worship at the church.

Dr. Gray is known to be an astute politician who has served on many boards and agencies and functioned as the Health Coordinator for the Memphis Affiliate of the Congress of National Black Churches for ten years.

He has served on the Tennessee Human Rights Commission under three governors. He is a published author and a mentor to many young pastors. I remember Leo Gray as an outspoken young man who cared about Lane College, his community, and those who had less than him. This fraternity man still exhibits these traits today.

Dr. John Odom
Alpha Phi Alpha Fraternity, Inc.

John Odom came to Lane College from the local high school, so his reputation preceded him. I remember conversations about his academic prowess. He was known to have a high level of confidence that some perceived as arrogance. But I am told that he always held his own in any setting. To this end, the yearbook shows that he became president of the Freshman class and Student Government Association representative for his sophomore class.

Odom was elected to Whos' Who Among students in American Colleges and Universities and completed his degree in three years. His leadership skills were evident from his freshman year and they never waned.

Dr. Odom proudly gives credit to Lane College for his career preparation and success. He cites Mabel Henderson, Dr. Robert G. Owens, Dr. J. O. McShine, and Ms. Edna W. Cawthorn as examples of teachers who poured into him untiringly.

Besides being an academic giant, Odom was known for his outstanding voice, oratory skills, acting ability, and for being a leading Alpha Man. I remember that he was a tenor soloist in my dad's concert choir. As a little girl I remember him singing in "The Messiah". The members of the choir usually came to our house for dinner after the program and he was always center stage. I am told that he acted in plays and represented Lane College at the local and national levels.

My dad told me that when Lambuth College (a private white college) approached Lane for a student to take the lead role in a musical they were producing after the death of Dr. Martin Luther King, Jr., John Odom was unanimously selected to represent Lane College.

During the 1968-69 academic year; Lane College experienced student riots. I remember hearing the adults speak about the uprising on the campus. John Odom, a student at the time collaborated with then president Dr. Kirkendoll to restore order to the campus. At the end of the 1969 school year, John was presented an award for "Courageous Christian Leadership and Future Promise in Christian Service". That award proved prophetic because over the years, Dr. Odom's talents and intellect have flourished as he became a highly successful public school and college teacher and administrator, worked tirelessly to advance the causes of equality and justice, and published three books that have received wide recognition and acclaim. His speaking, facilitation, and management skills inspired him to establish his own company, Odom and Associates, LLC, a human resource development firm where he has been President for 34 years.

In John Odom I saw a young man who was intelligent, bold, and energetic. Even as a fraternity man, he held on to his commitment to God, family, and equality for all. He still stands tall among men.

Dr. Cassandra Y. Owens

Mr. Donald W. Comer

Kappa Alpha Psi Fraternity, Inc.

When I think about Kappa and consider how a fraternity can nurture and undergird an individual to reach his full potential, I think of Donald Comer. I have known him all my life. He and my older brother are the same age. So much of the time when our paths crossed, he and Skip were engaged in some boyish activity while I would spend my time playing with his younger sister. Even then I knew he was destined to achieve great things as I quietly admired him from a distance.

Because we were family I do not have to stand on formality. I called him Don. While Don was a product of his environment. I noted early on that he was determined to not let his environment limit his potential. I have heard my mother say many a time, "that Don is just like his granddaddy Oliver."

Oliver Womack, my grandfather's first cousin. was a stalwart fixture of the Blairs Chapel community and if I could characterize him with two words, they would be compassionate and generous. Don inherited those traits and together they align to one of the key principles of Kappa. He says that is what drew him to the fraternity and keeps him tightly tethered there. "I learned early in my journey into Kappa-land the principle of ALTURISM, unselfish concern for the welfare of my brother. That resonated with me and solidified for me that the good ole Kappa Spirit and who I aspired to be are one and the same". Anyone who knows of Kappa knows that members declare their fundamental purpose to be ACHIEVEMENT and that Kappa does not make men, men make Kappa. Well Donald Comer, my cousin Don, is a Kappa man through and through and he epitomizes these principles. Now do not get me wrong. He does indeed have that Kappa SWAG that most of us have come to know and expect as well.

If you ask me what his gifts are, I'd have to say intellect and leadership. From his early years at Parkview Elementary school as a crossing guard and honor roll to his matriculation to West Senior High School where he was both senior class president and valedictorian, he has been on a continuous journey to manifest greatness. Even in 1978 his classmates saw his potential and proclaimed what was to come when they elected him most likely to succeed. But remember, I declared it first playing there in the dirt with his younger sister.

Don entered the University of Tennessee at Martin in Fall 1978. He very quickly distinguished himself and found himself immersed in leadership roles furthering the mission of the institution and enhancing his growth and development.

On campus he served in student government, the black student association and was appointed as an ambassador to the University of Tennessee system representing the Martin campus. Even today the University considers him to be a true success story and holds him out as a shining example of what is possible. As the institution, with all intentionality, looks to position itself as a welcoming and affirming educational stronghold, Don is a clear return on the school's investment in sustaining and growing a diverse and inclusive educational culture.

Today he is employed by FedEx, a Fortune 100 company and global economy bellwether. As Staff Vice President, Decision Science and Analytics, he leads a team that leverages cutting edge technologies including artificial intelligence and machine learning to guide the enterprise to make smart decisions. He helps keep FedEx at the forefront of data exploration to uncover insights that can reimagine and evolve the business and increase profitability.

Amidst his notable career success, he has not forgotten the many lessons that Kappa has and continues to teach him. He did not get where he is alone and while he may not be able to repay those who helped get him there, he is committed to paying it forward.

He proudly acknowledges the other officers, directors, managers and individual contributors who are a part of the FedEx enterprise. He personally curates' content to an internal distribution list of Kappa men titled "Kappa Achievement Alerts." The distribution celebrates achievement of his fellow Kappa's at FedEx, but more importantly offers information and support to feed their fascination for the business and foster the continued achievement of his fellow Kappa brothers.

Over the time that I have known him I have seen him amazingly negotiate the evolution that marks a life well lived, from learning to earning to returning. Now do not get me wrong, he is a continuous learner, but now he's leaning more heavily into returning. He often talks about the "give-back." Don has an unwavering passion to positively impact the lives of black people.

He gives of his time, talents and resources serving on the board of trustees at Lemoyne-Owen College, and Stillman College. Additionally, he chairs the National Black MBA Association Board. His commitment to excellence has been recognized across many platforms over his career as both a business leader and community activist.

As he looks forward, one word guides him, relevancy. He desires to stay relevant and points to his 2018 feature in Black Enterprise Magazine's as a Modern Man Honoree that he is having some modicum of success in doing just that.

Dr. Cassandra Y. Owens

Dr. Elias Blake

Alpha Phi Alpha Fraternity, Inc.

My final fraternity game changer, like the first, is one who impacted my life closely and from afar. Because of him and the institution he led with such astute zeal; I can meet most of the challenges that confront me as a professional today with confidence. He allowed me to see leadership in ways that I could not define at the time, but they still help me get through those times when moving forward is difficult.

I graduated high school and left my hometown of Jackson, TN to attend Clark College in Atlanta, GA. I spent a massive amount of time on the campus of Lane, so I knew I would attend a historically black college. But I wanted to be on my own, so I chose Clark College. I will never forget the day that my parents drove me to Atlanta and left me at Clark. My mom was sitting on the passenger side of their 1979 gray Caprice Classic with red velvet seats almost in tears. As my dad waved and drove away, I knew I had a choice on whether to sink or swim.

It was Freshman week; so, no upperclassmen were on campus except for freshman guides. The next week upperclassmen arrived on campus and began calling us "crabs" because we had not earned any academic hours. One of my first times walking to the cafeteria I intersected with a tall man that demanded my attention. It was a feeling I felt before, but I ignored it and ate my dinner. As the week progressed, I attended a Freshman Class assembly. The speaker was the same man I saw a couple of days before. I learned that he was the President of the college. His name was Dr. Elias Blake. As I sat in Haven Warren Davage Auditorium with its gray walls and red seats, I thought to myself, "he reminds me of Bishop C. A. Kirkendoll." I later learned that Dr. Elias Blake was also a member of Alpha Phi Alpha Fraternity.

Dr. Blake was a trailblazer in the Higher Education arena. He broke new ground advocating for equality of opportunity and access to higher education for African American students. In 1970, Blake published a study showing that 70% of all African Americans with bachelor's or graduate degrees were educated at historically black colleges. The report led to a meeting among President Richard Nixon and several college presidents and laid the foundation for amendments to the Federal Higher Education Act that expanded support for predominantly black colleges. It was a paradox, he said, that school integration resulting from the Supreme Court's landmark Brown vs. Board of Education decision of 1954 removed control of black schools from the black community. As a result, he said, expectations were lowered, and black students began to fall behind their white counterparts. During his 10-year presidency at Clark College, he oversaw a period of steady growth in enrollment, programmatic offerings including the launching of the mass communications program, and set the college on a sound financial path. He made major improvements in faculty training and curriculum securing national accreditations for academic programs. Blake played trumpet in his youth and was a lifelong lover of jazz.

He made jazz music a signature experience at WCLK radio on the campus of Clark College. Emerging as a national leader on higher education issues, he advised both United States Presidents Nixon and Carter on higher education issues, particularly the needs of Blacks in higher education.

His ability to relate at all levels, move the College forward, and understand the importance of the times made him an extraordinary Fraternity man.

Dr. Cassandra Y. Owens

CLARK COLLEGE FRATERNITY RECOGNITIONS

As I continued to matriculate at Clark and learned the Black Greek Lettered Organization culture, it became a large part of my academic experience. I want to pay homage to the membership intake lines at Clark College during my maturation process.

The Crimson Renaissance - Fall 80 Gamma Kappa Chapter- Kappa Alpha Psi Fraternity: Mr. Nicky Wimby, Mr. Derrick Holloway, Mr. David Carnegie, Mr. Anthony Felder, Pastor Doug Thompson, Dr. Harold Scott, Mr. Harvey Giddens, and Mr. Theodore Kelsick.

The Ten Most Wanted - Fall 81 Beta Psi Chapter – Omega Psi Phi Fraternity: Mr. Shawn Watson, Mr. Darryl Johnson, Mr. Harold Mathews, Mr. William Hardy, Mr. Willie Shivers, Mr. Andre Mitchell, Mr. Jeffery Jones, Mr. Dwayne Brown, Mr. Wilton Munnings, and Dr. Darryl Elzie.

GAME CHANGERS

The Ineffable Nine–Fall 81 Alpha Phi Chapter-Alpha Phi Alpha Fraternity: Mr. Sam Deshazior, Rev. Cord Franklin, Mr. Albert Amey, Mr. Gary Brown, Mr. Thomas Tatum, Mr. Edward Davis, Mr. Shelton West, Mr. Eddie Lewis, Mr. Curtis Flowers.

I enjoyed reflecting on the experiences that are a part of this chapter. I am hopeful that as you continue reading these pages, you were able to recall a memory from your journey that impacted your life. The men that are mentioned from my college years are still a rich part of my life. I look forward to seeing them at homecoming in Atlanta. I am also thankful for the men on these pages who impacted my life indirectly.

It is good to highlight men who understand purpose, destiny, and ethical behavior. It is my thought that fraternity life impacted their lives in positive ways, enhanced values, principles, and standards that are a significant part of who they were and are today. It is also my belief that most of the African American fraternity men on the college campuses today will be written about positively as they take their places as leaders in the years to come.

Perhaps, you see the stories I mentioned as isolated incidents. Maybe this was the first time you ever engaged with histories of unsung heroes of our times who happened to be men of color. It is my plight to establish as normal, professional, community committed, discipline, big hearted men who are men that are African American. My journey is not unique. It did not happen in isolation. Black men have been impacting communications through their fraternities for a century. Let's delve deeper.

DIFFERENCE MAKERS

4

By the mid-1800s, slavery was just beginning to end in the North but was still considered a way of life in the South. At this time, only 28 Blacks had received college degrees (Crump, 1991). African American students on college campuses did not have access to social or scholarly activities. Since the establishment of a Black fraternity, Alpha Phi Alpha, Incorporated, at Cornell University in 1906, institutions of higher education have struggled with a racially dichotomous Greek system. Fraternities were a big part of student life during that time at Cornell.

Black male students attending the institution in 1905 met together as a literary society to discuss current issues and create a forum for closer relations (Wesley, 1991). The era of Black fraternalism began 4 years before the founding of Alpha Phi Alpha Fraternity, Inc., which is recognized as the oldest historically Black college fraternity.

Often recognized as a precursor of Kappa Alpha Psi Fraternity, Inc., Alpha Kappa Nu Greek Society was founded in 1903 at Indiana University in Bloomington, Indiana. The founders of the organization were James Knight, Howard Thompson, E. B. Keemer, Fred Williamson, John Hodge, Thomas Reynolds, Mr. Hill, R. A. Roberts, and Gordon Merrill (Bryson, 2003). Dr. Henry Minton, a physician, envisioned an organization that mirrored the benefits he saw his white counterparts enjoying through membership in Greek-letter organizations (Kimbrough, 2003a).

On May 15, 1904, he along with Drs. E. C. Howard, A. B. Jackson, R. J. Warrick, E. T. Hinson, and R. J.Abele founded Sigma Pi Phi. This group was established as a graduate organization and the first elite club for Black men. Membership was extended unsuccessfully when the two undergraduate men died shortly of illness after initiation (Kimbrough, 2003a). Records indicated the existence of Pi Gamma Omicron and Gamma Phi Fraternities in the state of Ohio (Kimbrough, 2003b). An article was found in the Chicago Defender alluding to a Black Greek-letter organization on the campus of The Ohio State University. While these organizations were short lived, they played an important role in the history of Black Greek-letter organizations. With the founding of Alpha Phi Alpha in 1906, the era of Black fraternalism began and includes the founding of Kappa Alpha Psi, Omega Psi Phi, Phi Beta Sigma, and Iota Phi Theta fraternities.

Alpha Phi Alpha Fraternity, Inc. The campus climate at Cornell College (now Cornell University) mirrored that of the American society (Ross, 2000). During the fall semester of 1905, it should be noted that all six of the African American students from the 1904-1905 class did not return that following school term. This extremely low retention prompted students who would become the founders of Alpha Phi Alpha Fraternity, Inc. to create a study and support group for the college's remaining African American students (Ross, 2000). With the goal of encouraging each other in their academic and professional pursuits, this assembly came together to form a support group that became the foundation for what would become the oldest historically Black college fraternity. By the fall of 1906, the literary support group evolved into the Alpha Phi Alpha Society (Kimbrough, 2003a). On the afternoon of December 4, 1906, a motion was passed to form the first national college fraternity for Black men, Alpha Phi Alpha, Fraternity, Inc. The founders of Alpha Phi Alpha

Fraternity were Henry Arthur Callis, Eugene Kinckle Jones, Robert Harold Ogle, Charles Henry Chapman, Nathaniel Allison Murray, George Briddle Kelly, and Vertner Woodson Tandy (Ross, 2000). The fraternity was based on the ideals of manly deeds, scholarship, and love for all mankind (Ross, 2000).

Kappa Alpha Psi Fraternity, Inc. The story of Kappa Alpha Psi Fraternity, Inc. began at Howard University in 1910 where founders Elder Watson Diggs and Byron Kenneth Armstrong were originally enrolled (Bryson, 2003). When Diggs and Armstrong transferred to Indiana University in the fall of 1910, they found an environment that was not welcoming of African American students. The two men noted that they could go weeks without seeing another African American on campus. Like the environment experienced by the men who went on to found Alpha Phi Alpha Fraternity at Cornell, these conditions made assimilation into the campus culture nearly impossible. On the campus of Indiana University, African American students were denied use of recreational facilities and were not allowed to participate in contact sports. African American students were permitted to display their athletic prowess in track and field (Bryson, 2003). In a response to these conditions, nine men met at the home of Mollie Spaulding to create a temporary organization, Alpha Omega (Bryson, 2003). The group met again on January 5, 1911, the official founding date, and selected officers for the organization.

The group decided that the new fraternal organization would be based on Christian ideals and the fundamental purpose of achievement (Bryson, 2003). The new fraternity was named Kappa Alpha Nu Fraternity, Inc. (Crump, 1991). An historian for the fraternity recounted that the name was perhaps in tribute to the African American students who organized Alpha Kappa Nu Fraternity in 1903 to create a better life for themselves at Indiana University (Bryson, 2003). The application for incorporation was filed with the State of Indiana on April 11, 1911, with the signatures of Elder Watson Diggs, Ezra D. Alexander, Byron Kenneth Armstrong, Henry T. Asher, Marcus Peter Blakemore, Paul W. Caine, George W. Edmonds, Guy Levis Grant, Edward G. Irvin, John Milton Lee, and Frederick Mitchell. Frederick Mitchell withdrew from the university and did not return, thus never becoming a member of the organization.

The fraternity was incorporated on May 15, 1911 and is recognized as the first undergraduate fraternal organization to be incorporated by African Americans as a national body (Crump, 1991). From the inception, the fraternity never barred anyone from membership based on race, religion, or national origin (Bryson, 2003). The name was changed to Kappa Alpha Psi Fraternity, Inc., on April 15, 1915, as a result of a racial remark towards fraternity member Frank Summers as he was competing in a track and field event (Bryson, 2003; Crump, 1991; Ross, 2000).

Omega Psi Phi Fraternity, Inc. In response to the establishment of the second chapter of Alpha Phi Alpha, Omega Psi Phi Fraternity, Inc. was founded at Howard University (McKenzie, 1986). Omega Psi Phi was the first Black Greek Lettered Fraternity established on a historically black campus (Jeffries, 2008). On Friday, November 17, 1911, three best friends, Edgar Love, Oscar Cooper, and Frank Coleman, who were Howard University undergraduates, met in the office of Dr. Ernest Everett Just, a Howard biology professor (Ross, 2000). From the initials of the Greek phrase meaning "friendship is essential to the soul," the name Omega Psi Phi was derived (Jeffries, 2008). Omega Psi Phi Fraternity, Inc., was founded upon the principles of scholarship, manhood, perseverance, and uplift (Ross, 2000).

Initially, the newly established organization was met with opposition from the administration including Howard President Dr. Wilbur P. Thirkield (Ross, 2000). The men continued to push to make their vision come to fruition and gain recognition of their fraternity. After meeting with the administration and implementing suggested changes, the administration agreed to recognize the organization on the premise it would remain a local fraternity and not expand (Ross, 2000). After subsequent meetings with administration the fraternity was finally recognized as a national organization and incorporated in 1914 (Ross, 2000).

Phi Beta Sigma Fraternity, Inc. The idea to create another fraternity at Howard University began in the summer of 1910 in Memphis, Tennessee, when future founder and high school senior Abram Langston Taylor discussed Greek life on the campus of Howard with an alumnus (Hughey, 2008). Taylor had already been accepted to

Howard and wanted to organize a Greek letter fraternity that would truly exemplify the ideals of brotherhood, scholarship, and service. On January 9, 1914, Phi Beta Sigma Fraternity, Inc. was founded by Abram Langston Taylor, Leonard Francis Morse, and Charles Ignatius Brown. This group of men believed that potential members should be judged on their own merits and not on their affluence, skin tone, or texture of hair (Phi Beta Sigma, 2001). The fraternity motto is "Culture for Service and Service for Humanity" (Hughey 2008). The founding of Phi Beta Sigma Fraternity, Inc. would temporarily end the era of Black Greek fraternalism. As the fifth organization, Iota Phi Theta, Fraternity, Inc., would not be established until 1963.

GAME CHANGERS

Iota Phi Theta Fraternity, Inc. On September 19, 1963, at Morgan State College (now Morgan State University), 12 students founded what is now the nation's fifth largest, predominately African American social service fraternity: The Iota Phi Theta Fraternity, Incorporated.

The Honorable Founders of Iota Phi Theta were: Albert Hicks, Lonnie Spruill, Jr., Charles Briscoe, Frank Coakley, John Slade, Barron Willis, Webster Lewis, Charles Brown, Louis Hudnell, Charles Gregory, Elias Dorsey, Jr., and Michael Williams.

This group of men were unique for several reasons. First, many were long-time friends. Spruill, Coakley, Dorsey, and Gregory had known one another since grade school, and Spruill and Coakley's friendship extended to when the two were preschoolers. Even more uniquely, many of these men were what are now referred to as "Non-Traditional Students" and were 3-5 years older than the average college student. Gregory, Willis, and Brown were all service veterans, and Brown,

Hicks, and Briscoe were married with small children. Of this group of 12, several were also working full-time jobs, and all were full-time students.

Based upon their ages, heightened responsibilities, and increased level of maturity, this group had a slightly different perspective than the norm for college students. It was this perspective from which they established the Fraternity's purpose, "The development and perpetuation of Scholarship, Leadership, Citizenship, Fidelity, and Brotherhood among Men." Additionally, they conceived the Fraternity's motto, "Building a Tradition, Not Resting Upon One!"

The Fraternity functioned as a local entity until the first interest groups were established in 1967 at Hampton Institute (Beta Chapter) and Delaware State College (Gamma Chapter). Further expansion took place in 1968 with chapters being formed at Norfolk State College

(Delta Chapter) and Jersey City State College (Epsilon Chapter). The Fraternity was officially and legally incorporated on November 1, 1968 as a National Fraternity under the laws of the State of Maryland. Today, Iota Phi Theta consists of 249 chapters located in 40 States as well Japan, Korea and the Bahamas.

YOUNG, GIFTED & BLACK

5

In the first part of this book, I provide a historical perspective about black men who impacted this country while maintaining membership in prestigious black fraternities. Also, I wanted you to become more acquainted with each organization, while allowing you to get to know some of the great men that influenced my world.

However, the second part of this project is designed to gather data from and about individual young men who are currently in college and are a part of the fraternal organizations mentioned earlier. Each fraternity that I highlight designed a national position for their collegiate members. This position allows the collegiate to serve on the

National Board of Directors. This intergenerational comradery is beneficial in many aspects. Some of which I will highlight later.

I interviewed each collegiate member of their national organization for this next segment of research. Each of the young men interviewed for this segment holds this position.

While organizations vary in their title or description of the collegiate in this position, the person elected or selected to serve in this capacity is the highest-ranking collegiate member in the organization. This undergraduate office is usually designed for one who has demonstrated excellent leadership skills and has exhibited abilities and understanding of the goals of the organization. The intent of this phase of the book is to determine from the perspective of these identified college young men how the fraternity has affected their development and what they viewed as most important about their membership.

Mr. Evan Jackson

Kappa Alpha Psi Fraternity, Inc.

Mr. Evan Jackson Jr. serves as Grand Vice-Polemarch of Kappa Alpha Psi Fraternity, Inc. He is a member of Lambda Xi Chapter. He is currently a Junior at Brown University majoring in Economics and Religious Studies. His self-reported grade point average is 3.8.

Evan is a legacy as his father is a member of Kappa Alpha Psi and upon reflection he knows now that his father groomed him to follow in his footsteps during his childhood. Evan remembers fondly being around his dad and the other fraternity men so his decision to join Kappa was an easy one. He says that the Kappa men he knew as a child had dual personalities. They were able to handle the business of the organization and be extremely personable at the same time.

Evan was elected to his current position in Philadelphia at the 84th Grand Chapter Meeting. He was unopposed. His campaign platform was business development, which is not surprising as he is a business owner. However, he is also concerned about the intergenerational connection of the membership and how the brothers have access to one another. To that end, he was instrumental in the enhancement of the Achievement Academy Website. This website was designed to ensure that undergraduate members can interact with graduate brothers for mentoring or to get questions answered. Through his efforts, the website was redesigned and made more user friendly so that brothers could connect by profession, region, or interest. It provides another way for brothers to network.

Mr. Jackson identifies his leadership style as Influential with a sprinkle of Participative /Democratic.

He is charismatic, and uses persuasion, expertise, and authority to lead; but he also seeks information from the team before making final decisions.

He models his leadership style after the current Grand Polemarch, Mr. Reuben Shelton. Mr. Shelton has a way, according to Evan, that brings people in and makes them feel a part of the team. He thinks that Mr. Shelton blends charisma, influence, and authority in a smooth and unassuming way that leads Kappa men to meet their objectives.

His community service project is the "Hands on Book Program." This is a partnership with the non-profit Rooms to Read. He was featured on the NBC Today Show promoting this project. The project works because the men of Kappa Alpha Psi bring books to each provincial meeting. Then, the collegiate members visit local elementary schools in lower socio-economic areas and read the books to children and leave the books for the library. Now, Evan wanted to make sure that I understood that these books are culturally relevant.

The books are written in South Africa and highlight black people in a positive way.

Mr. Jackson is an entrepreneur; the owner of Intus Care located in Providence, RI. – a company that provides data-based healthcare technology solutions to long term care providers in order to improve care outcomes for the elderly. He wants to ensure that the quality of healthcare for older adults is best.

Evan plans to attend Business School after graduation. He wants the brothers to remember him and his administration as one who gave all he had to advance Kappa.

Mr. Dane Norvell, '99

Phi Beta Sigma Fraternity, Inc.

Mr. Dane Norvell is a first-generation college student attending the University of Memphis. He is a graduating senior with a 3.4 grade point average. He is a Political Science major with a minor in Africana Studies. He is a member of Delta Nu chapter. He was initiated into this fraternity in 2018 and he holds the position of International 2nd Vice-President. Dane has also held the position of Regional Vice-President, which is the highest-ranking collegiate position in the Region.

Dane came to the college with leadership skills. He was influenced by the college chapter president to seek membership in this fraternity. He believes that it is our responsibility to mentor someone to take our place. No one should leave a position without having trained someone to step in and keep the process moving. Dane is a born change agent. He has a hunger for leadership.

So, it is not surprising that he would seek the highest office in the fraternity. He ran his campaign from two acronyms: (1) ROOTS - Rights, Organizations, Oppression, Trends and Strengths. He created that acronym because of the narrative about the portrayal of black men in mainstream America. His second acronym is PLAN - Professional Development, Life Skills, Academic Skills, and Networking. He wants to empower the brothers to grow and develop into a productive populace through workshops that teach this competence in these areas. He is not just a leader in the fraternity, but as a child he was an Eagle Scout which possibly gave him his hunger for leadership. He is a member of the Mighty Sound of the South Marching Band, and the Pep Band where he is a trumpeter. Now, it is probably clear by now that he is Section Leader in the band because Mr. Norvell is a natural leader.

GAME CHANGERS

Dane identifies as a transformational/coaching leader. He will assist members in their endeavors, but he also wants members to own their responsibility in the process. As he trains or assists, he inspires his mentees with the following: "speak victory, claim victory and act victorious.", which has become his motto for living. He credits his fraternity with being the conduit for his continued growth and development. He believes that because he was willing to invest himself into this organization, he has reaped bountiful benefits.

Vice-President Norvell plans to attend graduate school after graduation. He plans to pursue his MBA and then a Juris Doctorate. He wants his administration to be remembered as one that allowed collegiate brothers to be their "best self". He provided a platform that allowed personal growth and development. He has a passion for helping people and seeing them obtain their goals and dreams.

Mr. Norvell is an entrepreneur, he is the owner of Lunchbox 901 93

A place where healthy meals are served. There are no fried foods except for the sides. Everything else is grilled at the establishment. He will always be grateful for the opportunity that Phi Beta Sigma Fraternity afforded him as he pursued his leadership endeavors.

Mr. Austin Tatum

Omega Psi Phi Fraternity, Inc.

Mr. Austin Tatum held the position of 2nd Vice-Grand Basileus of Omega Psi Phi Fraternity, Inc. from 2018-2020. Mr. Tatum is a graduate of Alcorn State University. He was inducted into Eta Chapter in 2016. His twin brother is also his membership intake brother. He majored in Biochemistry. Mr. Tatum thought he wanted to be a physician; but changed his mind and is now working on the master's in Healthcare Administration.

Mr. Tatum was elected to his current position at the 2018 Conclave in New Orleans. He had competition and his campaign platform was CARE- Collaborating with Undergraduates to Retain Enthusiasm. His community focus was health care initiatives. His administration encouraged collegiate brothers to support St. Jude Children's Research hospital, mental health, and Breast Cancer Awareness. His administration was also concerned with Voter Registration.

Mr. Tatum was also a leader on the campus of Alcorn State. He held the position of secretary of the Chemistry Club, a member of the campus Pan-Hellenic Council and was a member of the National Pan-Hellenic Council where he served as Parliamentarian. He plans is to own a Health Care facility in the future.

He believes that he has a Democratic leadership style. He is team oriented, always trying to keep the brothers involved and engaged.

He wants to be remembered as a transparent leader, a positive influence who embraces the uniqueness of each person, a brother that puts the needs of Omega first and always seeking the best interest of the fraternity.

Mr. Kendall Brooks

Iota Phi Theta Fraternity, Inc.

Books is currently serving as the 2nd Grand Polaris of Iota Phi Theta Fraternity, Inc. Mr. Brooks was inducted into the Alpha Lambda Chapter at the University of Illinois at Urbana-Champaign. He is a first-generation college student and as an undergraduate he was a Political Science major. He is now matriculating to receive the Master of Business Management degree. Brooks was a member of the reactivation membership intake that took place Fall 2019.

GAME CHANGERS

Mr. Brooks was appointed to the position by the Grand Polaris, George Smith, Jr., because he noticed his dynamic leadership abilities as he attended different activities throughout the fraternity. He was drawn to this fraternity because he believes that campus culture influences which fraternity is selected for membership. He felt that the employees at his institution who were members of Iota exhibited the values and principles that he identified with and thus wanted to become a member of their fraternity.

In his current position, his community focus project will be police brutality and civil disobedience. His leadership style is Influence as he uses his charisma to encourage people and inspire them to best their best self. He focuses on individual relationships and making sure that each brother embraces differences and feels valued and appreciated.

Mr. Brooks was a leader prior to joining Iota as is evident by the following: he was a member and president of Men of Impact, Student Senator, Tutor, Resident Assistant and Business Consultant. He wants his administration to be remembered as one that emphasized proper planning; strategic preparation and learning how to present oneself as a man of character. In fact, he emphasized that the same man you are in the dark is the same man you should be in the light. His future aspirations are to be an entrepreneur, and eventually serve this country in the political arena as a US Congressman.

Mr. Russell Williams, III

Alpha Phi Alpha Fraternity, Inc.

Alpha Phi Alpha Fraternity's administrative structure is different from the other fraternities. Five Regional Assistant Vice Presidents comprise their collegiate leadership. Each of them represents a Region and they all have a seat on the National Board. The current Assistant Vice Presidents are Travis Nelson, East; Jonathan A. Moore, Midwest; DeMarcus Johnson, South; Russell R. Williams, Southwest; and Grant A. Frink, West.

These gentlemen are expected to exemplify the excellent characteristics that should be evident in all collegiate brothers.

Mr. Russell Williams, III, who is the representative from the Southwestern Region, was interviewed for this book project.

Mr. Williams joined Alpha Phi Alpha Fraternity in 2016 and was inducted into the Beta Chi Chapter at Philander Smith College.

He was a Political Science Major with a final grade point average of 3.5. Mr. Williams also wears the title of National Collegiate Brother of the Year.

According to Mr. Williams, he chose Alpha because of the friendship of the brothers on the Philander Smith campus. Also, his high school principal, Dr. Rodney Johnson, is a member of Alpha Phi Alpha. He stated that this fraternity taught him how to develop personal and professional relationships and the value of uplifting his community and the brotherhood. Another positive gain from fraternity membership was that it exposed him to many wonderful opportunities for personal and professional growth and development. His community service foci are education and political awareness.

Mr. Williams knows he is naturally drawn to leadership. He has served Alpha at every level.

He was also elected to the office of District Assistant Vice-President before serving on the National Board.

When he sought the office of Regional Assistant Vice-President his campaign platform was FOCUS- Financial Literacy, Opportunity, Commitment, Unity, Success. He had strong competition when he sought the position. However, he emerged victorious and has learned from and enjoyed the experience.

On the campus of Philander Smith, Mr. Williams has held several elected and appointed leadership roles. He has served as Student Government Vice-President and President, 2016 White House Initiative HBCU All-star, and 2017 LH McCord Ambassador.

Based on his experience as a leader Mr. Williams describes his leadership style as transformative with a bit of influential.

Mr. Williams believes that black fraternities are still needed today because they provide a unique perspective and can produce change and be change agents in our communities. Fraternities can develop strategic plans that can open new doors for the first time and place different people at tables where they have never sat before.

He wants to be remembered as a Vice-President who listened, presented new ideas, and was not afraid to include all brothers at the table. He has future aspirations of receiving the Juris Doctorate as well as a master's degree in Public Service.

His goal is to be active in the political arena. He wants to serve his city and state as a political force.

Dr. Dorsey Miller

Omega Psi Phi Fraternity

The highest ranking elective undergraduate position on the Supreme Council of Omega Psi Phi Fraternity is Second Grand Vice Basileus.

The leadership of this organization shows an outstanding list of collegiate contributors, but the focus of this project was to define current collegiate fraternity leadership. However, it was determined that there is a member of Omega Psi Phi Fraternity who was elected to serve as Second Vice Basileus as an undergraduate.

He continued the Omega journey after graduation. He held several national leadership positions and was subsequently elected to the Office of Grand Basileus. He is the only member of the organization with this distinction.

It was my delight to have a conversation with Dr. Dorsey Miller who holds the distinction of being 2nd Vice-President as a collegiate and Grand Basileus as a graduate brother. Mr. Miller followed Mr. Jesse Jackson as 2nd Vice-President of Omega Psi Phi Fraternity.

Dr. Miller was inducted into the Psi Chapter at Morehouse College in 1962.

Dr. Cassandra Y. Owens

He was elected 2nd Vice-President at the 1964 Conclave held in Denver, CO.

He does not remember his campaign platform but remembers that he had three opponents for the position at the Conclave. He enjoyed the leadership role he was able to assume, and the learning experiences gained from interacting with the members of the Supreme Council.

Representing the college brothers across the nation was an awesome responsibility and served as a steppingstone to later achievements.

Dr. Miller was elected to Grand Basileus at the Cleveland Conclave in 1994 and he served until 1998. His administration was a moving and shaking one. Some of his accomplishments were:

- Moving the headquarters from Washington, DC to Decatur, GA (outside of Atlanta)
- Establishing the Endowed Chair positions at Historically Black Colleges
- Introduced a four-year strategic plan for the fraternity
- Created social action programs

- Formed the Project for the Perpetuation of the Black Male
- Developed Foster Grandparents – A program where Omega Men invested in Senior Citizens
- Initiated conversations to establish Heath Care Facilities in Soweto, South Africa (he left office before that became a reality)
- Omega men were one of the first organizations to participate in Habitat for Humanity

Dr. Miller believes that black fraternities are still needed today. He says these are one of the organizations that remain under the control of black people. The young men today need positive role models and fraternity men could and should be the answer.

Dr. Miller closed our conversation with these words: "one of our unwritten cardinal principles is respect for womanhood." As a female I embraced those words, because that is one of the things, I remembered about the men in the Atlanta University Center.

Remember, Mr. Miller is a Morehouse Man and I attended Clark Atlanta University. As we talked, we reminisced although we attended different schools, the Center was family.

I remembered fondly, young men who would not use certain language in my presence; open the door for me, or who indirectly by some action made me feel respected, valued, and appreciated.

I salute, Past Grand Basileus Miller, and am thankful to him and each of them taking time to speak with me.

RESEARCH & DATA

6

This chapter describes the demographic data regarding the participants in the study that inspired this book. The study was based on existing, secondary data retrieved from the National Survey of Student Engagement. The NSSE data was used with the permission from the Indiana University Center for Postsecondary Research. I am including this data so that the reader will know that this is not my opinion, but that the numbers demonstrate the accomplishments that Black men have achieved during their collegiate years and beyond.

This chapter contains data related to testing the research hypotheses that were used during my study.

Research Hypotheses

1. There is a significant difference in the development of leadership skills for African American males at Historically Black Colleges involved in fraternities compared to African American males not in fraternities at Historically Black Colleges.

2. There is a significant difference in academic success for the African American males involved in fraternities at Historically Black Colleges compared to African American males not involved in fraternities at Historically Black Colleges.

3. There is a significant difference in the quality of interactions with other students for African American males at Historically Black Colleges involved in fraternities compared to African American males not in fraternities at Historically Black Colleges.

4. There is a significant difference in the quality of interactions with faculty for African American males at Historically Black Colleges involved in fraternities compared to African American males not in fraternities at Historically Black Colleges.

5.   There is a significant difference in the quality of interactions with staff for African American males at Historically Black Colleges involved in fraternities compared to African American males not in fraternities at Historically Black Colleges.

The Indiana University Center for Postsecondary Research is the overseer of the National Survey of Student Engagement. The Report was used to collect the data necessary for this study. A Web-based version and paper version of The Report was available to students.

The study was conducted with existing, secondary data obtained from the National Survey of Student Engagement from 15 institutions from the southeastern section of the United States. The sample consisted of African American males who were enrolled in private HBCUs. The states that make up this population were Alabama, Florida, Georgia, Tennessee, and South Carolina. The state of Mississippi was requested; however, there was no data from that state. The sample size was 866 male respondents.

Statistical Results

Research Hypothesis 1: There is a significant difference in the development of leadership skills for African American males at Historically Black Colleges involved in fraternities compared to African American males not involved in fraternities at Historically Black Colleges.

A total of 648 males responded to both questions of leadership development and fraternity involvement. Results indicated a significant difference in African American male students who were members of a fraternity. They were more likely to develop leadership skills (M = 3.569) than those who were not fraternity members (M = 2.793).

Research Hypothesis 2: There is a significant difference in academic success for African American males involved in fraternities at Historically Black Colleges compared to African

American males not involved in fraternities at Historically Black Colleges.

A total of 468 students were included in this analysis. These students reported both their grades and membership in fraternity. The information was used to test this hypothesis.

Although these results did not show significance, those males who were fraternity members reported higher grades (M = 5.662) than did those who were not fraternity members (M = 5.343).

Research Hypothesis 3: There is a significant difference in the quality of interactions with other students for African American males involved in fraternities at Historically Black Colleges compared to African American males not involved in fraternities at Historically Black Colleges.

A total of 637 students responded to the question of quality of interaction with students and fraternity membership. Those who were fraternity members were significantly more likely to report more positive quality of interaction with students

(M = 6.138) than were non-fraternity members (M = 5.724).

Research Hypothesis 4: There is a significant difference in the quality of interactions with faculty for African American males involved in fraternities at Historically Black Colleges compared to African American males not involved in fraternities at Historically Black Colleges.

Students who responded to fraternity membership and quality of interaction with faculty totaled 629. Males who were fraternity members were significantly more likely to report positive interaction with faculty (M = 6.683) than non-fraternity members (M = 5.279).

Research Hypothesis 5: There is a significant difference in the quality of interactions with staff for African American males involved in fraternities at Historically Black Colleges compared to African American males not involved in fraternities at Historically Black Colleges.

Students who responded to both fraternity membership and interaction with staff totaled 591. The results indicated no significant difference between the two groups of the quality of interaction with staff. However, those males who were members of a fraternity reported more positive interaction with staff (M = 5.111) than non-fraternity members interaction with staff (M = 4.830).

In conclusion, the data indicated that the young men who were involved in fraternities were leaders on their campus. I am pleased to present this data to you as an academic indicator of the great things that African American males achieve that have been largely impacted by their organizational status.

Dr. Cassandra Y. Owens

CONCLUSION

The purpose of this book is to highlight the impact that membership in fraternities has on leadership development skills, academic success and involvement with peers, faculty and staff for African American male students attending Historically Black Colleges in the Southeastern United States. The catalyst for this book is to respond to existing limitations in the literature in capturing a narrative explanation behind the direct relationship membership in fraternities has on student success.

It should be noted that male students who have established a record of involvement in campus organizations earned the trust and admiration of their peers (as determined by holding a leadership role or roles in their fraternity) and developed quality relationships with Greek-letter advisors and campus administration.

The concept of "being a Black fraternity man" proved to have a profound impact on fraternity members and how it correlates with student success and leadership development. Membership in fraternities creates a sense of responsibility to represent not only all Black men but also the Black fraternities on campus.

These young men view themselves as examples of how all Black men should be viewed on campus given their involvement on campus and in the spotlight. Given its label, they felt the pressure to excel academically, maintain professional and respectable mannerisms, and be socially engaging in the eyes of their Greek and non-Greek peers, faculty, and administration.

Fraternity members have a sense of "mattering." Schlossberg (1989) noted that many things can divide us culturally and can leave some populations feeling marginalized. Mattering is the belief that we matter to someone else (Schlossberg, 1989). At this core, fraternities create a sense of mattering for their members. They create a family environment where members can thrive and grow with others who share similar values.

For African Americans, the village concept rings true. The village can and must take different shapes, sizes, and forms. One of its forms for men is the fraternity.

Clearly this village has produced men who are extraordinary leaders, great fathers, and strong community activists.

In closing, despite the images and stories that the majority of those across the globe receive about black men, I wanted to be sure to insert a true history of who they are and what they represent. Black men are and have always been significant figures in their families, their communities, and industries. My prayer is that the truth about the success of black men becomes mainstream.

APPENDIX A:CULTURAL GAME CHANGERS

I could not end this book without mentioning some black men that are not members of fraternities but made a lasting impact on our lives. These men have made significant contributions to Black society and our communities. The trajectory of our lives has changed in ways that we all can acknowledge because of these Black Men. There are others that should be on this list; you may have others to add; I hope that you do. My list is in the succeeding pages below.

Dr. Cassandra Y. Owens

NAME	AREA OF IMPACT
Mr. Emmitt Till	Martyr
Mr. Trayvon Martin	Martyr
Mr. Fred Hampton	Black Panther Party
Mr. Stokely Carmichael	Black Panther Party
Mr. H. Rap Brown	Black Panther Party
Mr. Malcolm X	Politics
Ice Cube	Entertainment
Dr. Dre	Entertainment
Mr. Doug E. Fresh	Entertainment
Mr. Stevie Wonder	Entertainment
Mr. Will Packard	Entertainment
Mr. Tyler Perry	Entertainment
Mr. D. L. Hughley	Comedian
Mr. Chris Rock	Comedian
Mr. Kirk Franklin	Gospel
Rev. T.D. Jakes	Religion
Mr. Jermain Dupree	Producer
Mr. Spike Lee	Entertainment
Mr. Andre Harrell	Entertainment
Mr. Lebron James	Sports
Mr. Arthur Ashe	Sports
Rev. Frederick Eikerenkoetter	Religion

GAME CHANGERS

Mr. James Brown	Entertainment
Mr. Jim Brown	Sports
Mr. Julius "Dr. J." Erving	Sports
Mr. Stephen Curry	Sports
Mr. Makur Maker	Sports
Mr. Marvin Ellison	CEO Loews
Mr. Donnie Simpson	Entertainment

The greatest non-fraternity black man of all time is: The 44th United States President Barack H. Obama.

Dr. Cassandra Y. Owens

APPENDIX B:PRESIDENT OF HISTORICALLY
BLACK COLLEGES & UNIVERSITIES

INSTITUTIONS	PERSON	ORGANIZATON
Allen University	Dr. Ernest C. McNealy	Alpha Phi Alpha
Bethune-Cookman	Dr. E. LaBrent Chrite	Alpha Phi Alpha
Clafin University	Dr. Dwaun J. Warmack	Kappa Alpha Psi
Clark Atlanta University	Dr. George T. French, Jr	Alpha Phi Alpha
Dillard University	Dr. Walter M. Kimbrough	Alpha Phi Alpha
Fisk University	Dr. Vann Newkirk	Phi Beta Sigma
Florida Memorial University	Dr. Jaffus Hardrick	Alpha Phi Alpha
Johnson C. Smith	Mr. Clarence D. Armbrister, J.D.	Alpha Phi Alpha
Lane College	Dr. Logan C. Hampton	Alpha Phi Alpha
Livingstone College	Dr. Jimmy R. Jenkins, Sr.	Omega Psi Phi
Morris College	Dr. Leroy Staggers	Alpha Phi Alpha
Philander Smith	Dr. Roderick L. Smothers, Sr.	Alpha Phi Alpha
Rust College	Dr. David L. Beckley	Omega Psi Phi

Dr. Cassandra Y. Owens

INSTITUTIONS	PERSON	ORGANIZATION
Talladega College	Dr. Billy C. Hawkins	Omega Psi Phi
Virginia Union University	Dr. Hakim J. Lucas	Alpha Phi Alpha
Voorhees College	Dr. W. Franklin Evans	Alpha Phi Alpha
Wilberforce University	Dr. Elfred Anthony Pinkard	Alpha Phi Alpha

Other President Who Were Not Members of Fraternities

Dr. A Zachery Faison-Edward -**Waters College**

Dr. Lester Newman- **Jarvis Christian College**

Dr. David A. Thomas-**Morehouse College**

Dr. Leslie Pollard- **Oakwood College**

Dr. Dwight Fennell-**Texas College**

REFERENCES

Albritton, T. J. (2012). Educating our own: The historical legacy of HBCUs and their relevance for educating a new generation of leaders. *Urban Review: Issues And Ideas In Public Education, 44*(3), 311-331.

Bryson, R. J. (2003). *The story of Kappa Alpha Psi: A history of the beginning and development of a college Greek letter organization 1911-1999* (5th ed.). Philadelphia, PA: The Grand Chapter of the Kappa Alpha Psi Fraternity.

Crump, W. L. (1991). *The story of Kappa Alpha Psi*. Philadelphia, PA: Kappa Alpha Psi Fraternity.

Graham, L. (1999). *Our kind of people: Inside America's Black upper class*. New York, New York: Harper.

Harper, S. R. (2008). The effects of sorority and fraternity membership on class participation and African American student engagement in predominantly Whiteclassroom environments. *College Student Affairs Journal, 27*(1), 94-115. http://dx.doi.org/10.1353/ihe.2006.0053.

Hughey, M. W. (2008). Constitutionally bound: The founders of Phi Beta Sigma fraternity and Zeta Phi Beta sorority. In G. S. Parks (Ed.), *Black Greek-letter organizations in the 21st century: Our fight has just begun* (pp. 95-114). Lexington, KY: The University Press of Kentucky.

Jeffries, J. L. (2008). The last shall be first: The founders of Omega Psi Phi fraternity. In G. S. Parks (Ed.), *Black Greek-letter organizations in the 21st century: Our fight has just begun* (pp. 67-74). Lexington, KY: The University Press of Kentucky.

Kimbrough, W. M. (2003a). *Black Greek 101: The Culture, Customs, and Challenges of Black fraternities and sororities*. Cranbury, NJ: Associated University Presses.

Kimbrough, W. M. (2003b). Historically Black fraternal organizations. In D. E. Gregory (Ed.), *The administration of fraternal organizations on North American campus: A pattern of the new millennium* (pp. 77-94). Asheville, NC: College Administration Publications.

Kuh, G.D., Pascarella, E. T., Wechhsler, H. (1996). The questionable value of fraternities. *The Chronicle of Higher Education*, Retrieved December 5, 2017 from www.chronicle of higher education.

McClure, S. M. (2006b). Voluntary association membership: Black Greek men on a predominantly White campus. *Journal of Higher Education, 77*(6), 1036-1057.

McKenzie, A. (1986). *Fraters: Black Greek-letter fraternities at four historically Black colleges*. (Doctoral Dissertation, Columbia University Teachers College, 1986). Digital Dissertations Database, 1920-1960. (UMI No. 8620386).

Noguera, P. A. (2003). The trouble with Black boys: The role and influence of environmental and cultural factors on the academic performance of African American males. *Urban Education, 38*, 431-459. doi:10.1177/0042085903038004005

Nuwer, H. (1999). *Wrongs of Passage: Fraternities, Sororities, Hazing, and Binge Drinking*. Bloomington, IN: Indiana University.

Ross, L. C., Jr. (2000). *The Divine Nine: The history of African American fraternities and sororities*. New York, NY: Kensington.

Schlossberg, N. (1989). Marginality and mattering: Key issues in building community.*New Directions for Student Services, 48*, 5-13. doi:10.1002/ss.37119894803.

Wesley, C. H. (1991). *The history of Alpha Phi Alpha: A development in college life*(15th ed.). Chicago: The Foundation Publishers. doi:10.2307/2714015

Dr. Cassandra Y. Owens

About the Author

Dr. Cassandra Y. Owens is

Department Chair and Assistant Professor of Religion at Lane College in Jackson, TN. She has also held professorial and administrative positions at Rust College, Holly Springs, MS; Macon College, Macon, GA; Fayetteville State University, Fayetteville, NC and Clark Atlanta University, Atlanta, GA. Higher education is her passion and believes deeply that "every student is worth the time and effort."

She holds degrees from Clark Atlanta University, Interdenominational Theological Center of Atlanta, GA, and Union University, Jackson, TN. She has membership in the following organizations: The American Association of Blacks in Higher Education, The American Association of University Women, Tennessee Association for Student Success and Retention, Association of Fraternity/Sorority Advisors, Sigma Gamma Rho Sorority, Inc. Toastmasters International; the NAACP, and Code Red Ministers Coalition. She is the immediate past Chairperson of the Faculty and Faculty Representative to the Board of Trustees at Lane College.

Dr. Cassandra Y. Owens

Contact Author

GAME CHANGERS

Want to schedule a book signing or speaking event with the author?

Complete the contact form at
www.drcassandraowens.com

Do You Want to Write a Book?

Contact our publisher at
www.drnesintl.com